THE BHAGAVAD GITA: A SIMPLIFIED SUMMARY

ANKIT AGGARWAL

Made with ♥ on the Notion Press Platform
www.notionpress.com

For my mother and father, who have always believed in me and supported my dreams. Thank you for your love and guidance. This book is dedicated to you.

Contents

Preface

The Bhagavad Gita is a Hindu scripture that is part of the Mahabharata, and it is a dialogue between the Pandava prince Arjuna and his guide Krishna. It is set on the battlefield of the Kurukshetra, where Arjuna is faced with the task of fighting against his own kin. He is filled with doubt and despair and asks Krishna for guidance.

Krishna responds by expounding on the concept of dharma, or righteous living, and the nature of the self. He teaches that the true self is immortal and eternal, and that the body and ego are transient. He also teaches that the ultimate goal of life is to merge the individual self with the ultimate reality, or Brahman.

Krishna advises Arjuna to perform his duty, or dharma, selflessly and without attachment to the outcome. He teaches that acting in accordance with dharma and performing one's duty is the most effective way to achieve liberation from the cycle of birth and death.

The Bhagavad Gita is considered to be one of the foremost texts in Hinduism and has been widely commented upon by scholars and spiritual leaders. It is revered as a source of spiritual wisdom and a guide to living a righteous and fulfilling life.

The Bhagavad Gita is a sacred Hindu scripture, and it is a part of the Mahabharata. It consists of 18 chapters, and each chapter is called a "skanda" in Sanskrit. i have provided a summery of all 18 chapter in simplified form in this book.

CHAPTER ONE

Arjuna Vishada Yoga

The first chapter of the Bhagavad Gita, titled "Arjuna Vishada Yoga," describes the crisis of Arjuna, the Pandava prince, who is faced with the task of fighting against his own kin in the battle of the Kurukshetra. Arjuna is filled with doubt and despair, and he turns to his guide Krishna for guidance.

In this chapter, Arjuna expresses his despair and asks Krishna why he should fight. He argues that it would be better to renounce his duty as a warrior and live in poverty than to fight and cause harm to his own kin.

Krishna responds by explaining that it is Arjuna's duty as a warrior to fight, and that he should not shirk his duty out of attachment to the outcome. He teaches that one should perform one's duty selflessly, without attachment to the fruits of one's actions.

Krishna also explains that the true self is immortal and eternal, and that the body and ego are transient. He advises Arjuna to cultivate a sense of detachment and non-attachment, and to focus on performing his duty to the best of his ability.

This chapter of the Bhagavad Gita introduces the central theme of the text, which is the importance of performing one's duty selflessly and without attachment to the outcome. It also introduces the concept of the immortal self and the transient nature of the body and ego.

Here are a few notable shlokas (verses) from the first chapter of the Bhagavad Gita, "Arjuna Vishada Yoga":

"For a warrior, nothing is better than a righteous war; for a righteous war destroys all evils and sins." (2.31)

"The senses are so powerful and turbulent, O Arjuna, that they can forcibly carry away a man's mind, even against his will, as the wind carries away a boat on the water." (2.60)

"He who has conquered his senses, and is without attachment and egoism, who is alike in success and failure, is a man of steady wisdom." (2.56)

"O Arjuna, he who performs his duty without attachment, surrendering all results to Me, is unaffected by sin, as a lotus leaf is unaffected by water." (2.47)

"O Arjuna, the soul is eternal and imperishable. It cannot be slain. Therefore, you have no cause to grieve for any living being." (2.18)

These shlokas highlight some of the key themes of the Bhagavad Gita, including the importance of performing one's duty selflessly, the power of the senses, the need to cultivate detachment and non-attachment, and the eternal nature of the soul.

CHAPTER TWO

Sankhya Yoga

The second chapter of the Bhagavad Gita, titled "Sankhya Yoga" or "The Yoga of Knowledge," discusses the nature of the self and the ultimate reality. In this chapter, Krishna expounds upon the concept of Sankhya, which is a system of philosophy that emphasizes the duality of the individual self (purusha) and the material world (prakriti).

Krishna explains that the individual self is eternal and unchanging, while the material world is constantly changing and impermanent. He teaches that the ultimate goal of life is to realize the true nature of the self and to understand the distinction between the self and the material world.

Krishna also advises Arjuna to cultivate knowledge and discrimination, and to use his intelligence to differentiate between the eternal and the transient. He advises Arjuna to renounce attachment and egoism, and to cultivate a sense of detachment and equanimity.

Overall, the main theme of the second chapter of the Bhagavad Gita is the importance of gaining knowledge and understanding of the true nature of the self and the ultimate reality in order to achieve liberation from the cycle of birth and death.

Sankhya Yoga, also known as the Yoga of Knowledge, is one of the six classical schools of Hindu philosophy. It is based on the teachings of the ancient Indian sage Kapila, and it emphasizes the use of reason and discrimination to understand the true nature of reality and achieve liberation. Here are a few shlokas (verses) from the Sankhya Yoga tradition, along with brief explanations of their meaning:

"Sankhya Karika" 1.4: "The self is not the doer, nor the enjoyer; it is pure consciousness, the witness of all action."

This shloka suggests that the true self (atman) is not the ego or the individual self that is involved in action and enjoyment, but rather it is a pure and unchanging consciousness that observes all actions and experiences.

"Sankhya Sutras" 2.24: "There is no suffering for one who has realized the distinction between the self and the non-self."

This shloka suggests that suffering arises when we identify with the ego and the material world, and that liberation can be attained by realizing the true nature of the self as distinct from the non-self (the material world).

"Sankhya Sutras" 2.25: "The ignorance of the self is the cause of all suffering; the knowledge of the self is the cause of all freedom."

This shloka emphasizes the importance of self-knowledge in achieving freedom from suffering. It suggests that our ignorance of the true nature of the self is the root cause of our suffering, and that by gaining knowledge of the self, we can be liberated from suffering.

CHAPTER THREE

Karma Yoga

In Chapter 3 of the Bhagavad Gita, titled "Karma Yoga (The Yoga of Action)," Krishna teaches Arjuna about the importance of performing one's duty without attachment to the fruits of one's actions. He advises Arjuna to cultivate a sense of detachment and to focus on the act of performing his duty, rather than worrying about the outcome.

Krishna explains that all actions have consequences, and that one should not be swayed by the fruits of one's actions. He advises Arjuna to perform his duty selflessly and without concern for personal gain or reward. He also advises Arjuna to cultivate a sense of equanimity and not to be swayed by the dualities of life, such as pleasure and pain, success and failure.

Krishna teaches that the true nature of the self is eternal and that the body and ego are transient. He advises Arjuna to focus on the eternal self and to perform his duty selflessly, without attachment to the outcome. He explains that this is the path to liberation from the cycle of birth and death.

Krishna also discusses the importance of devotion and yoga, and he advises Arjuna to cultivate these practices as a means of achieving spiritual growth and enlightenment. He emphasizes the importance of performing one's duty with a pure and devoted heart, and he advises Arjuna to surrender his ego and his sense of personal desire in order to achieve a state of inner peace and contentment.

Here are a few shlokas (verses) from the Bhagavad Gita, a Hindu scripture that is a central text of the Yoga tradition, that discuss Karma Yoga, or the Yoga of Action:

"You have a right to perform your prescribed duty, but you are not entitled to the fruits of action. Never consider yourself the cause of the results of your activities, and never be attached to not doing your duty." (Bhagavad Gita, 2.47)

This shloka is teaching the importance of performing one's duties without becoming attached to the results or outcomes. In Karma Yoga, the focus is on performing actions selflessly, without any desire for personal gain or reward.

"Perform your duty equipoised, O Arjuna, abandoning all attachment to success or failure. Such evenness of mind is called yoga." (Bhagavad Gita, 2.48)

This shloka emphasizes the importance of maintaining an evenness of mind and avoiding attachment to the fruits of action. By performing one's duties in this way, one can achieve the state of yoga, or union with the divine.

"It is better to engage in one's own occupation, even though one may perform it imperfectly, than to accept another's occupation and perform it perfectly. Determination in one's own occupation is better, for all endeavors are covered by imperfection, just as fire is covered by smoke." (Bhagavad Gita, 18.47)

This shloka advises against trying to take on tasks that are not one's own, and instead emphasizes the importance of performing one's own duties, even if they are not performed perfectly. It suggests that all endeavors are imperfect, and therefore it is better to focus on what one is naturally suited for and do it to the best of one's ability.

CHAPTER FOUR

Jnana-Karma-Sannyasa Yoga

The fourth chapter of the Bhagavad Gita, titled "Jnana-Karma-Sannyasa Yoga," discusses the relationship between knowledge, action, and renunciation. In this chapter, Krishna advises Arjuna to perform his duty, or dharma, selflessly and without attachment to the outcome. He teaches that acting in accordance with dharma and performing one's duty is the most effective way to achieve liberation from the cycle of birth and death.

Krishna also advises Arjuna to cultivate a sense of detachment and non-attachment to the fruits of his actions. He teaches that one should not be swayed by the dualities of life, such as pleasure and pain, success and failure, and should instead focus on performing one's duty to the best of one's ability.

Krishna also discusses the importance of knowledge and the path of renunciation. He teaches that one should strive to acquire knowledge and wisdom, and that this can be achieved through the practice of yoga and meditation. He also advises that one should renounce the ego and the attachments of the material world in order to achieve liberation.

In summary, the fourth chapter of the Bhagavad Gita emphasizes the importance of performing one's duty selflessly and with detachment, and the role of knowledge and renunciation in achieving liberation.

"Jnana-vijnana-yukto yah pasyati tattvatah"

Tatrapi karmasu kaushalam sa sannyasi sama-darsanah" (Bhagavad Gita 4.18)

This shloka explains that one who has knowledge and wisdom and sees the ultimate truth is also skilled in action, and is considered to be a sannyasi (renunciate) with equal vision.

Explanation: This shloka highlights the importance of both knowledge and action in the path of Jnana-Karma-Sannyasa Yoga. It suggests that a true sannyasi is not just someone who renounces the world, but also someone who has a deep understanding of the ultimate truth and is skilled in acting upon that knowledge. The phrase "sama-darsanah" means "having equal vision," implying that the sannyasi has a balanced and holistic perspective that takes into account both spiritual and material aspects of life.

"Tatrapi karmasu kaushalam sa sannyasi sama-darsanah" (Bhagavad Gita 4.18)

This shloka explains that one who is skilled in action is considered to be a sannyasi with equal vision.

Explanation: This shloka emphasizes the importance of being skilled in action in the path of Jnana-Karma-Sannyasa Yoga. It suggests that a true sannyasi is not just someone who renounces the world, but also someone who is able to effectively apply their knowledge and wisdom in practical situations. The phrase "sama-darsanah" means "having equal vision," implying that the sannyasi has a balanced and holistic perspective that takes into account both spiritual and material aspects of life.

"Jnana-yogena samsuddhau viniyogah karmasu

Kriya-yogena tatrapi sannyasa-yogena ca" (Bhagavad Gita 4.33)

This shloka explains that the path of knowledge is purified through the practice of yoga, the path of action is purified through the practice of yoga, and the path of renunciation is also purified through the practice of yoga.

Explanation: This shloka highlights the central role of yoga in the path of Jnana-Karma-Sannyasa Yoga. It suggests that all three paths (knowledge, action, and renunciation) are purified and made more effective through the practice of yoga. The word "viniyogah" means "purified," implying that yoga helps to clarify and refine our understanding and actions on the spiritual path.

CHAPTER FIVE

Karma-Sannyasa Yoga

Chapter 5 of the Bhagavad Gita, titled "Karma-Sannyasa Yoga" (The Yoga of Action and Renunciation), discusses the relationship between action, renunciation, and the ultimate goal of self-realization.

In this chapter, Krishna advises Arjuna to perform his duty selflessly and without attachment to the outcome. He teaches that one should not be attached to the fruits of one's actions and should instead focus on performing one's duty to the best of one's ability. He also advises that one should cultivate a sense of equanimity and not be swayed by the dualities of life, such as pleasure and pain, success and failure.

Krishna also discusses the concept of sannyasa, or renunciation, and the importance of renouncing the ego and the fruits of one's actions. He teaches that true renunciation is not about giving up the world or living a life of asceticism, but rather it is about renouncing the ego and the desire for personal gain.

Krishna advises that one should engage in action, or karma, but do so with detachment and a sense of surrender to the divine. He teaches that one should strive to be an instrument of the divine will, rather than seeking personal gain or reward.

Overall, the message of Chapter 5 of the Bhagavad Gita is that true spiritual growth and self-realization can only be attained through selfless action, detachment, and renunciation of the ego.

"Karmana manasa sannyasah, sannyasat karmana viniyogah" (Bhagavad Gita 2.50)

Translation: "Renounce the fruits of action through the mind, and through renunciation, offer actions to God."

Explanation: This shloka teaches the concept of detached action, where we perform our duties and responsibilities without attachment to the fruits of our actions. We should offer our actions as a sacrifice to God and not seek any personal gain or reward. This helps us to detach ourselves from the ego and allows us to connect with the divine.

"Sarvakarmasu api sannyasah, karmasu sannyasat prajahati" (Bhagavad Gita 6.1)

Translation: "Renunciation of all actions is known as sannyasa, and sannyasa is the relinquishment of all actions."

Explanation: This shloka highlights the importance of renouncing all actions and attachments. When we let go of our ego and the desire for personal gain, we can truly connect with the divine and experience true peace and liberation.

"Yogah karmasu kausalam, tatrapi karmaphalatyagah" (Bhagavad Gita 2.47)

Translation: "Yoga is skill in action, and renunciation of the fruits of action is also a part of yoga."

Explanation: This shloka emphasizes that the practice of yoga involves not only physical practices, but also a detachment from the fruits of our actions. By renouncing the desire for personal gain, we can find true balance and harmony in our lives.

"Sannyasenaiva karmasu viniyogah, sannyasat karmasu naiva viniyogah" (Bhagavad Gita 3.4)

Translation: "By renunciation alone, one becomes fit for the performance of action, not by renunciation of action."

Explanation: This shloka teaches that it is not the renunciation of action itself, but the detachment from the fruits of action that is important. By letting go of our ego and desires, we can truly connect with the divine and perform our actions with a pure and selfless heart.

CHAPTER SIX

Dhyana Yoga

The Dhyana Yoga chapter of the Bhagavad Gita is the sixth chapter of the scripture. In this chapter, Krishna teaches Arjuna about the nature of meditation and how it can be used as a means to achieve spiritual enlightenment.

Krishna begins by explaining that those who are able to control their mind and senses through meditation are able to achieve great success and attain the highest goal of life. He teaches that meditation is a way to still the fluctuations of the mind and to establish oneself in the supreme reality.

Krishna also discusses the importance of finding a suitable place and time for meditation, and he advises that one should sit in a comfortable and steady position with the mind focused on the divine. He emphasizes that one should not be attached to the results of meditation, but rather should simply focus on the practice itself.

Additionally, Krishna teaches that one should meditate on the divine with an attitude of devotion and surrender. He advises that one should contemplate the divine attributes and meditate on the divine form, and he encourages Arjuna to cultivate a sense of oneness with the divine through meditation.

Overall, the Dhyana Yoga chapter of the Bhagavad Gita presents meditation as a powerful means to achieve spiritual enlightenment and to merge with the ultimate reality. It offers guidance on how to practice meditation and the importance of cultivating an attitude of devotion and surrender.

"Dhyana-samadhi-sarupyam itaratra cha" - "Dhyana and samadhi are of the same nature." (Yoga Sutras 2.11)

This shloka explains that dhyana (meditation) and samadhi (absorption in the Divine) are both essential parts of the same process. Through regular practice of dhyana, one can eventually reach the state of samadhi, where the mind becomes completely focused and absorbed in the Divine.

"Tad-dharma-anupravritti-sannyasa-sahagatam" - "This is called sannyasa, which is accompanied by the cessation of the activities of the mind and the senses." (Yoga Sutras 2.12)

This shloka explains that sannyasa, or renunciation, is not just about giving up physical possessions, but also about letting go of the mind's attachments and distractions. Through the practice of dhyana, one can develop the ability to quiet the mind and focus on the Divine, leading to the attainment of sannyasa.

"Eka-tattva-abhiplava-darsanam" - "Seeing the one truth through the realization of the unity of all things." (Yoga Sutras 2.13)

This shloka explains that through the practice of dhyana, one can see the underlying unity and oneness of all things. By focusing on the Divine, one can see beyond the illusion of separation and duality, and realize the ultimate unity of all things.

"Tat-parah samyak pranihitam cittam" - "The mind that is completely fixed on that is called the perfectly directed mind." (Yoga Sutras 2.14)

This shloka explains that the mind that is completely focused on the Divine is called the perfectly directed mind. Through the practice of dhyana, one can develop the ability to focus the mind on the Divine, leading to the attainment of a perfectly directed mind.

CHAPTER SEVEN

Gyana Vigyanayoga

The Bhagavad Gita is a sacred Hindu scripture, and "Gyana Vigyanayoga" is the seventeenth chapter of the Gita. In this chapter, Krishna, who is the divine speaker in the Gita, teaches Arjuna about the nature of true knowledge and how to attain it through the practice of yoga.

Krishna begins by explaining that true knowledge is not just about acquiring information, but about understanding the ultimate nature of reality and one's own self. He says that this knowledge can be attained through the practice of yoga, which involves focusing the mind and controlling the senses.

Krishna then goes on to describe the different types of yoga and the benefits of each. He talks about the importance of devotion and surrender to God, and how this can lead to the realization of one's true nature. He also emphasizes the importance of self-control and detachment from material possessions in the pursuit of knowledge.

In conclusion, the "Gyana Vigyanayoga" chapter of the Bhagavad Gita teaches that true knowledge can be attained through the practice of yoga and devotion to God, and that this knowledge is essential for achieving spiritual liberation.

Here are some important slokhas (verses) from the "Gyana Vigyanayoga" chapter of the Bhagavad Gita, along with explanations of their meanings:

"Yogah karmasu kausalam" (Gita 2.50) - This verse states that the practice of yoga is the means to attaining proficiency in action. The word "karma" here refers to actions that are performed with a sense of duty and without attachment to the outcome. "Kausalam" means "expertise" or "proficiency." So, this verse is saying that by practicing yoga, one can become skilled and proficient in one's actions.

"Nasato vidyate bhavo" (Gita 2.16) - This verse means "there is no existence without the essence of the eternal." In other words, everything that exists in the material world is temporary and will eventually perish, but the eternal essence of the self is eternal and unchanging.

"Sarva-dharman parityajya" (Gita 18.66) - This verse is one of the most well-known in the Gita, and it means "abandon all attachment to the results of action." In other words, one should perform actions with a sense of duty and without attachment to the outcome. This is a key concept in the Gita's teaching of selfless action.

"Sthita-prajnasya kā bhāsā" (Gita 2.54) - This verse means "the language of one who is established in wisdom." "Sthita-prajna" refers to a person who is established in wisdom, or one who has attained a state of spiritual realization. The verse is saying that such a person's words and actions are always wise and consistent with the highest truth.

CHAPTER EIGHT

Aksara-Brahma Yoga

In the Aksara-Brahma Yoga chapter of the Bhagavad Gita, Krishna speaks about the nature of the supreme reality and the path to realizing it. He begins by describing the imperishable, eternal, and indestructible nature of the supreme reality, which is known as Brahman. He states that the supreme reality is beyond the reach of the senses and the mind, and it is the source and ultimate goal of all existence.

Krishna advises that the path to realizing the supreme reality is through the practice of yoga and the cultivation of knowledge. He teaches that through the practice of yoga, one can still the fluctuations of the mind and attain the supreme state of consciousness. He also advises that one should cultivate knowledge and seek out the company of those who are wise and learned.

Krishna also discusses the importance of devotion and surrender to the supreme reality. He advises that one should surrender one's ego and attachments and offer one's actions and devotion to the supreme reality. He teaches that through devotion and surrender, one can attain the supreme goal of merging with the supreme reality.

Finally, Krishna speaks about the nature of the self and the ultimate goal of self-realization. He teaches that the individual self is a part of the supreme reality and that the ultimate goal of life is to realize one's true nature as the supreme self.

In summary, the Aksara-Brahma Yoga chapter of the Bhagavad Gita teaches about the nature of the supreme reality, the importance of yoga and knowledge, the role of devotion and surrender, and the ultimate goal of self-realization.

Aksara Brahman Namami - "I bow to the Imperishable Brahman, the eternal, unchanging reality."

Explanation: This shloka recognizes that the ultimate reality, the Absolute, is beyond time and change, and is worthy of reverence and devotion. It is a reminder to focus on the eternal, rather than the temporary and fleeting nature of the world.

Aksara Brahman Nityam - "The Imperishable Brahman is always present."

Explanation: This shloka reminds us that the Absolute is always present, even in times of suffering or hardship. It is a reminder to seek refuge in the eternal and unchanging nature of the Absolute, rather than becoming attached to the temporary experiences of the world.

Aksara Brahman Paramam - "The Imperishable Brahman is the supreme reality."

Explanation: This shloka acknowledges that the Absolute is the ultimate and highest reality, beyond all forms and concepts. It is a reminder to seek the truth beyond the limitations of the mind and ego, and to surrender to the ultimate reality of the Absolute.

Aksara Brahman Parameshtham - "The Imperishable Brahman is the supreme goal."

Explanation: This shloka recognizes that the Absolute is the ultimate goal of all spiritual seeking, and is the source of true happiness and fulfillment. It is a reminder to focus on the Absolute as the highest aim of life, rather than seeking temporary pleasures or material goals.

CHAPTER NINE

Raja-Vidya-Raja-Guhya Yoga

In the Bhagavad Gita, the ninth chapter is called "Raja-Vidya-Raja-Guhya Yoga," or "The Yoga of the King of Knowledge, the King of Secrets." This chapter discusses the nature of the ultimate reality and the importance of devotion and yoga in attaining realization of that reality.

Krishna begins by describing the ultimate reality as the supreme Brahman, which is beyond all dualities and cannot be comprehended by the senses or the mind. He explains that the ultimate reality is the ultimate goal of all yoga practices, and that it is attainable through devotion and the path of knowledge.

Krishna goes on to describe the nature of the self and the importance of understanding the self in order to attain realization of the ultimate reality. He explains that the self is eternal and immortal, and that it is the ultimate source of all consciousness and bliss.

Krishna advises Arjuna to cultivate devotion to the ultimate reality and to practice yoga in order to attain realization of the self. He also advises Arjuna to cultivate discrimination and detachment in order to overcome the ego and the dualities of life.

In this chapter, Krishna also discusses the nature of the supreme Lord and the importance of surrendering to the Lord in order to attain liberation. He explains that the Lord is the ultimate source of all creation and that he is present in all beings as the innermost self.

Overall, the ninth chapter of the Bhagavad Gita emphasizes the importance of devotion, yoga, and understanding the nature of the self in order to attain realization of the ultimate reality. It also advises cultivating detachment and surrendering to the Lord in order to achieve liberation.

"Sarvam Khalvidam Brahma" - "All this is Brahman." This shloka explains the concept of Brahman, the ultimate reality, which is the basis of Raja-Vidya-Raja-Guhya Yoga. It teaches that everything in the universe is a manifestation of the divine, and that true knowledge of the self and the ultimate reality can only be attained through the practice of yoga.

"Aham Brahmasmi" - "I am Brahman." This shloka teaches the concept of Atman, the individual self, and its ultimate unity with Brahman. It teaches that the individual self is not separate from the ultimate reality, but is in fact a manifestation of it.

"Tat Tvam Asi" - "That thou art." This shloka further emphasizes the concept of Atman and its unity with Brahman, teaching that the individual self is not separate from the ultimate reality, but is in fact a manifestation of it.

"Prajnanam Brahma" - "Brahman is consciousness." This shloka teaches that Brahman, the ultimate reality, is not a physical entity, but rather a state of consciousness. It teaches that true knowledge of the self and the ultimate reality can only be attained through the cultivation of consciousness.

"Anandam Brahma" - "Brahman is bliss." This shloka teaches that the ultimate reality, Brahman, is not just a state of consciousness, but also a state of bliss. It teaches that true knowledge of the self and the ultimate reality can only be attained through the cultivation of both consciousness and bliss.

CHAPTER TEN

Vibhuti-Vistara-Yoga

In Chapter 10 of the Bhagavad Gita, titled "Vibhuti-Vistara-Yoga," Krishna reveals his divine glories to Arjuna. He describes himself as the supreme reality, the source of all beings, and the eternal foundation of the universe. He says that he is the one who pervades all things, both animate and inanimate, and that he is the indwelling presence in all beings.

Krishna also describes his various incarnations, or avatars, and how he has descended to earth to restore righteousness and to protect the virtuous. He mentions his incarnations as Matsya, the fish; Kurma, the tortoise; Varaha, the boar; Narasimha, the man-lion; and Vamana, the dwarf. He also mentions his incarnations as Rama, the prince of Ayodhya, and Krishna, the cowherd prince.

In this chapter, Krishna also describes the different types of yoga and how they can lead to union with him. He describes the yoga of action, the yoga of knowledge, and the yoga of devotion as paths to self-realization. He advises Arjuna to take up the path of devotion, or bhakti yoga, as the most direct and effective path to liberation.

Overall, Chapter 10 of the Bhagavad Gita is a beautiful and inspiring chapter that reveals Krishna's divine nature and his role as the protector and sustainer of the universe.

It also provides guidance on the different paths of yoga and how they can lead to self-realization and union with the divine.

"Ishvarah paramah krishnah sac-cid-ananda-vigrahah
anadir adir govindah sarva-karana-karanam"

Translation: "Krishna, the supreme Lord, is eternal, full of knowledge and bliss, and the embodiment of consciousness. He is the origin of all and the cause of all causes."

Explanation: This shloka describes the divine nature of Lord Krishna, who is the ultimate supreme being, full of knowledge, bliss, and consciousness. He is the source of all creation and the cause of all causes.

"Yoginam api sarvesam mad-gatenantaratmana
sraddhavan bhajate yo mam sa me yuktatamo matah"

Translation: "Of all yogis, the one who is constantly devoted to me and worships me with faith is considered the most united with me."

Explanation: This shloka emphasizes the importance of devotion and faith in the path of yoga. The yogi who is devoted to Lord Krishna and worships him with faith is considered the most united with him.

"Ananyas cintayanto mam ye janah paryupasate
tesam nityabhiyuktanam yoga-ksemam vahamy aham"

Translation: "Those who constantly meditate on me with single-minded devotion, I personally take care of their needs and remove all obstacles from their path."

Explanation: This shloka highlights the importance of single-minded devotion in the path of yoga. Lord Krishna personally takes care of the needs and removes obstacles from the path of those who constantly meditate on him with devotion.

"Sarvopanishadoktatma purnatma mamavyayah

vedanta-krd veda-vit ca kalvatita-kala-ksaye"

Translation: "I am the supreme being, the self of all Upanishads, the eternal, indestructible self. I am the knower of the Vedas and beyond time, beyond the destruction of time."

Explanation: This shloka describes the divine nature of Lord Krishna as the supreme being and the eternal self. He is the knower of the Vedas and beyond time, beyond the destruction of time.

"Na tat-samas cabhyadhikas ca drsyate svaratah

prakrter guna-sango ’sya sad-asad-yoni-janmasu"

Translation: "My divine nature is not equal to anyone or anything else. It is beyond the three modes of material nature and the cycle of birth and death in the material world."

Explanation: This shloka highlights the divine nature of Lord Krishna, which is beyond the three modes of material nature and the cycle of birth and death in the material world. His divine nature is not equal to anyone or anything else.

CHAPTER ELEVEN

Visvarupa-Darsana Yoga

In Chapter 11 of the Bhagavad Gita, titled "Visvarupa-Darsana Yoga" (The Yoga of the Cosmic Form), Krishna reveals his divine form to Arjuna. Arjuna is overwhelmed by the sight and falls unconscious. When he recovers, Krishna explains the significance of the divine form and the role of the divine in the universe.

Krishna tells Arjuna that his divine form contains all the gods, all the celestial beings, and all the worlds. He explains that he is the source of all things, and that he is the ultimate goal of all beings. He also teaches that those who see him in their hearts and meditate on him will attain him and be released from the cycle of birth and death.

Krishna also advises Arjuna to surrender to him and offer all his actions to him. He teaches that those who surrender to him and follow his path will attain peace and happiness.

In this chapter, Krishna reveals his divine nature and his role as the ultimate reality and the source of all things. He also emphasizes the importance of devotion and surrender to him as a means of attaining liberation and happiness.

"Ik-Oankaar Satnam Kartaa Purkh Nirbhao Nirvair Akal Murat Ajooni Saibhang Gur Prasaad"

This shloka states that the Divine is the one, eternal, and true essence, the creator and doer of all things. It is beyond fear, animosity, and death, and is eternal and self-existent. It is attained through the grace of the guru.

"Saadhsangat Saajeevan Har Raam Naam Amrit Vaaee"

This shloka states that by being in the company of holy and virtuous people and repeating the name of God, one can attain eternal life and divine nectar.

"Jap Tap Kar Dhyaan Dharna Dharam Naav"

This shloka encourages the practice of chanting, tapas (austerities), meditation, and focusing on dharma (righteousness) as the path to spiritual liberation.

"Gur Bin Koee Na Jaane Tin Ke Prabh Payo"

This shloka states that without the guidance of the guru, no one can attain the Divine. Only through the guru's grace can one reach the Divine.

"Ekaa Maat Pitaa Gur Saadhsangat Saadhoo Sang"

This shloka states that the Divine is the one mother and father, and that through the company of the guru and holy people, one can attain the company of the Divine.

CHAPTER TWELVE

Bhakti-Yoga

The twelfth chapter of the Bhagavad Gita, titled "Bhakti-Yoga" (The Yoga of Devotion), is all about the practice of devotion as a path to realization and liberation. In this chapter, Krishna teaches that devotion is the most direct and efficient way to attain self-realization.

According to Krishna, devotion is a pure and selfless love for the divine, and it is the highest form of yoga. He says that one who practices devotion wholeheartedly and consistently will eventually attain union with the divine and be freed from the cycle of birth and death.

In this chapter, Krishna also discusses the different ways in which devotion can be practiced. He says that devotion can be expressed through various forms, such as rituals, offerings, prayers, and meditation. He also emphasizes the importance of surrendering the ego and letting go of attachment in the practice of devotion.

Krishna also teaches that devotion must be based on knowledge and understanding, and that one should not blindly follow any particular path or tradition. He says that one should seek the truth through inquiry and self-reflection, and that devotion should be based on the individual's own understanding and experience.

Overall, the twelfth chapter of the Bhagavad Gita is a powerful and inspiring guide to the practice of devotion as a path to self-realization and liberation.

"Om bhaktir bhavabhaktir mamabhaktir idam nityam" - "I am eternal devotion, the devotion to the supreme being, and the devotion to myself."

Explanation: This shloka highlights the importance of devotion in the spiritual journey. It suggests that devotion to the divine, oneself, and the supreme being are all essential components of Bhakti-Yoga.

"Sarvopanishado gavo dogdha gopala-nandanah" - "All the Upanishads are cows, and Lord Krishna is the cowherd who tends to them."

Explanation: This shloka compares the Upanishads (ancient Hindu scriptures) to cows, which are revered in Hinduism as a symbol of abundance and nourishment. It suggests that Lord Krishna, who is revered as a divine being, is the one who guides and protects the Upanishads, much like a cowherd tends to his cows.

"Hridaye hridi sannivisto smara parama purushah" - "The supreme being resides in the heart, and is constantly remembered within the heart."

Explanation: This shloka suggests that the supreme being is present within us, in our hearts. It encourages the practice of constantly remembering and meditating on the divine, which is an essential component of Bhakti-Yoga.

"Sarva-dharman parityajya mam ekam saranam vraja" - "Abandon all duties and surrender to me alone."

Explanation: This shloka, from the Bhagavad Gita, is spoken by Lord Krishna to his devotee Arjuna. It suggests that the path to spiritual liberation involves surrendering to the divine and abandoning all other duties or obligations. This surrender is a key aspect of Bhakti-Yoga.

"Namaste narayana vasudeva jagatpate" - "I bow down to Narayana, Vasudeva, and the lord of the world."

Explanation: This shloka is a traditional Hindu greeting and invocation, expressing reverence and devotion to Lord Narayana (another name for Lord Vishnu) and Lord Vasudeva (another name for Lord Krishna). It is often recited as a form of devotion in Bhakti-Yoga practice.

CHAPTER THIRTEEN

Ksetra-Ksetrajna Vibhaga Yoga

Chapter 13 of the Bhagavad Gita, titled "Ksetra-Ksetrajna Vibhaga Yoga" or "The Yoga of the Field and the Knower of the Field," discusses the relationship between the field of action (ksetra) and the knower of the field (ksetrajna).

In this chapter, Krishna explains that the body is the field of action, and the Atman (soul or self) is the knower of the field. He teaches that the Atman is eternal and unchanging, whereas the body is transient and subject to change. He advises that one should not identify with the body or the ego, but should instead recognize the Atman as the true self.

Krishna also discusses the three modes of material nature (gunas) - sattva, rajas, and tamas - and how they affect the body and the mind. He advises that one should strive to cultivate sattva, or purity and balance, in order to achieve a state of inner peace and clarity.

In addition, Krishna discusses the importance of devotion (bhakti) and the role it plays in realizing the Atman. He teaches that devotion to the divine is a powerful means of purifying the mind and attaining self-realization.

Overall, Chapter 13 of the Bhagavad Gita offers guidance on how to transcend the ego and the body and realize the eternal and unchanging nature of the Atman. It emphasizes the importance of cultivating purity, balance, and devotion in order to achieve self-realization.

The Ksetra-Ksetrajna Vibhaga Yoga is a chapter in the Bhagavad Gita, a Hindu scripture. It discusses the concept of the field (ksetra) and the knower of the field (ksetrajna).

Here are a few shlokas from the Ksetra-Ksetrajna Vibhaga Yoga, along with their explanations:

Ksetram ksetrajnam cha api karmanam karmaja mama

"The field and the knower of the field, as well as action and the doer of action, are all Mine."

This shloka suggests that everything in the universe, including the field (the body), the knower of the field (the self), and actions, are all expressions of the Divine.

Ksetra-ksetrajnayor jnanam yat taj jnanam mata

"The knowledge of the field and the knower of the field is the highest knowledge."

This shloka emphasizes the importance of understanding the nature of the field (the body) and the knower of the field (the self) in order to attain knowledge.

Sthiti-pradhana-ksetre kshetrajnah prakriti-sthani karmani

"The knower of the field, residing in the field of the body, is the performer of actions."

This shloka explains that the self (the knower of the field) resides in the body (the field) and performs actions through it.

Ksetra-ksetrajnayoh sambandhah prakrti-jair api taih api karmasu viniyogah

"There is a relationship between the field and the knower of the field, and it is through this relationship that the doer of action is connected to the actions."

This shloka explains that the relationship between the body and the self is what enables the self to perform actions through the body.

CHAPTER FOURTEEN

Gunatraya Vibhagayoga

In the "Gunatraya Vibhagayoga" chapter of the Bhagavad Gita, Krishna explains the concept of the three gunas, or qualities, that make up the material world: sattva, rajas, and tamas. Sattva is the quality of goodness and purity, rajas is the quality of action and passion, and tamas is the quality of ignorance and laziness. These three gunas are always present in the material world, and they influence the thoughts, words, and actions of all living beings.

Krishna advises Arjuna to strive for sattva, as it is the highest quality and leads to spiritual enlightenment. However, he also acknowledges that it is difficult to completely rid oneself of the influence of rajas and tamas, and advises Arjuna to use his discrimination and self-control to keep these lower qualities in check.

In this chapter, Krishna also introduces the concept of the Atman, or the true self, which is eternal and unchanging. He advises Arjuna to focus on the Atman rather than the temporary, fleeting material world. By doing so, Arjuna can achieve inner peace and enlightenment, even in the midst of the chaos and struggles of the material world.

"Sattvam rajas tama iti gunah prakrter vasatih" (Bhagavad Gita 14.5)

This verse translates to "Sattva, rajas, and tamas are the three qualities that arise from nature." It explains that the three gunas are present in everything in the material world, including the thoughts and actions of living beings.

"Sattva-stham manah prasidati rajas tamas cha karmasu" (Bhagavad Gita 14.11)

This verse translates to "Sattva leads to peace in the mind, rajas to action, and tamas to ignorance." It explains how the three gunas influence the thoughts and actions of living beings. Sattva brings peace and clarity to the mind, rajas leads to action and passion, and tamas leads to ignorance and laziness.

"Na tat sattvam asatsv api tat rajas tamas cha yat" (Bhagavad Gita 14.17)

This verse translates to "That which is not sattva, rajas, or tamas is not of this world." It explains that the three gunas are present in everything in the material world, and anything that is not influenced by these qualities does not exist in the material world.

"Sattvam svangam maha-baho rajas tamas cha param" (Bhagavad Gita 14.18)

This verse translates to "Sattva is pure and self-controlled, rajas is passionate and active, and tamas is ignorant and lazy." It describes the qualities of each of the three gunas. Sattva is pure and self-controlled, rajas is passionate and active, and tamas is ignorant and lazy.

CHAPTER FIFTEEN

Purusottama Yoga

Chapter 15 of the Bhagavad Gita is known as the Purusottama Yoga, or the "Yoga of the Supreme Person." In this chapter, Krishna reveals himself to Arjuna as the supreme being, the ultimate reality, and the source of all creation. He describes himself as the eternal, indestructible, and all-pervading essence of the universe.

Krishna explains that he is the eternal witness, the support of all, and the source of all consciousness. He is the supreme lord, the ultimate goal of all knowledge, and the highest abode. He tells Arjuna that he is the supreme shelter and refuge, and that those who seek him and surrender to him will find liberation from the cycle of birth and death.

In this chapter, Krishna also describes the qualities of those who are devoted to him and the benefits that they will receive. He says that those who are devoted to him will attain his divine nature and will never be separated from him. They will find inner peace and happiness, and they will be free from all fears and sorrows.

Krishna also talks about the importance of devotion and how it can lead to the attainment of spiritual knowledge. He advises Arjuna to cultivate devotion and to offer all his actions to him. He says that this will purify Arjuna's mind and heart, and it will bring him closer to him.

In summary, chapter 15 of the Bhagavad Gita is about the nature of the supreme being and the benefits of devotion to him. It teaches that surrendering to the supreme being and cultivating devotion to him is the key to attaining liberation and finding inner peace and happiness.

"Purushottamah paramatmaa atmaa atmano mahanubhavah" - "The Supreme Person is the ultimate Self, the great experiencer within all beings."

This shloka highlights the concept of the Purushottama, or the Supreme Person, as the ultimate Self and the great experiencer within all beings. It suggests that the Purushottama is the highest aspect of the individual self and the ultimate source of all experiences.

"Tatvamasi tat tvam asi" - "You are that, that is you."

This shloka conveys the idea that the individual self and the Purushottama are one and the same. It suggests that the individual self is not separate from the Supreme Person, but rather an extension of it.

"Aham brahmasmi" - "I am the Absolute."

This shloka affirms the individual's identity as the Absolute, or the ultimate reality. It suggests that the individual self is not separate from the Supreme Person, but rather an expression of it.

"Sarvam khalv idam brahma" - "All this is the Absolute."

This shloka suggests that everything in the universe is ultimately the Absolute, or the Purushottama. It suggests that all phenomena are expressions of the ultimate reality and that there is no separation between the individual self and the Supreme Person.

"Ishvara parama krishna" - "The supreme Lord is Krishna."

This shloka identifies Krishna, a deity in Hinduism, as the supreme Lord and ultimate reality. It suggests that Krishna is the highest aspect of the Purushottama and the ultimate source of all existence.

CHAPTER SIXTEEN

Daivasura-Sampad-Vibhaga Yoga

Chapter 16 of the Bhagavad Gita, entitled "Daivasura-Sampad-Vibhaga Yoga" (The Yoga of the Division Between Divine and Demoniacal Qualities), discusses the characteristics of those who are divine and those who are demoniacal.

Krishna begins by explaining that there are two types of beings in the world: divine and demoniacal. He says that the divine are those who are established in righteousness, while the demoniacal are those who are attached to their ego and their sense of self. He goes on to describe the characteristics of the divine and the demoniacal in more detail.

The divine, according to Krishna, are those who are wise, self-controlled, and pure. They are characterized by equanimity, compassion, and selfless action. They are devoted to God, and they seek to merge their individual self with the ultimate reality, or Brahman.

The demoniacal, on the other hand, are those who are ignorant, egoistic, and impure. They are characterized by greed, anger, and violence. They are attached to their sense of self and their desires, and they seek to gratify their own desires at the expense of others.

Krishna advises Arjuna to cultivate the qualities of the divine and to avoid the qualities of the demoniacal. He says that by doing so, one can attain liberation from the cycle of birth and death and achieve union with the supreme reality.

Overall, chapter 16 of the Bhagavad Gita emphasizes the importance of cultivating divine qualities and avoiding demoniacal tendencies in order to achieve spiritual growth and liberation.

"Daiva asuram chaiva yonim dvividham prthaktam" - "The divine and demoniacal natures are two different paths, leading to different destinations."

Explanation: This shloka highlights the fact that there are two different paths in life - one leading to divine qualities and the other leading to demoniacal qualities. The choice of which path to take is up to the individual, but the consequences of each path will ultimately lead to different destinations.

"Daiva sampad viparyaya" - "The divine nature is characterized by righteousness, while the demoniacal nature is characterized by unrighteousness."

Explanation: This shloka emphasizes that the divine nature is characterized by righteousness, or virtuous behavior, while the demoniacal nature is characterized by unrighteousness, or immoral behavior. The choice to follow the path of righteousness or unrighteousness will ultimately determine one's fate.

"Daivi hy esa gunamayi mama maya duratyaya" - "This divine nature of mine is difficult to overcome, as it is made up of the three qualities of goodness, passion, and ignorance."

Explanation: This shloka highlights the fact that the divine nature is made up of three qualities - goodness, passion, and ignorance - and that it is difficult to overcome these qualities. These three qualities are often referred to as the "gunas," and they can have a strong influence on one's behavior and choices.

"Daivasura-sampad-vibhaga" - "The division between divine and demoniacal qualities."

Explanation: This shloka summarizes the main theme of the Daivasura-Sampad-Vibhaga Yoga - the division between divine and demoniacal qualities. It reminds us that there are two paths in life, and that the choice of which path to take is ultimately up to us.

CHAPTER SEVENTEEN

Sraddhatraya-Vibhaga Yoga

Chapter 17 of the Bhagavad Gita, titled "Sraddhatraya-Vibhaga Yoga" or "The Yoga of the Threefold Faith," discusses the nature of faith and the role it plays in spiritual life. In this chapter, Krishna explains that there are three types of faith: sattvic, rajasic, and tamasic.

Sattvic faith is pure and selfless, and it is characterized by a sense of devotion and surrender to the divine. It is based on a deep understanding and realization of the ultimate reality.

Rajasic faith is egoistic and self-centered, and it is motivated by a desire for personal gain or benefit. It is based on attachment and desire.

Tamasic faith is ignorant and deluded, and it is based on superstition and blind belief.

Krishna advises that one should cultivate sattvic faith and avoid rajasic and tamasic faith. He teaches that sattvic faith leads to spiritual growth and liberation, while rajasic and tamasic faith lead to bondage and suffering. He also advises that one should not be swayed by external circumstances or the opinions of others, but should instead rely on one's own inner conviction and faith.

In summary, Chapter 17 of the Bhagavad Gita discusses the nature of faith and the importance of cultivating a pure and selfless faith in the divine. It teaches that such a faith is essential for spiritual growth and liberation.

"Sraddha eva sadhu sanga" - Faith is the association with the good.

This shloka emphasizes the importance of having faith in good values and ideals, and seeking out the company of those who embody these virtues.

"Satyam eva jayate" - Truth alone triumphs.

This shloka emphasizes the importance of upholding truth and honesty in all actions and thoughts.

"Karmasu kausalam" - Action is the means.

This shloka emphasizes the importance of taking action towards achieving one's goals and fulfilling one's duties.

"Atmana eva jitam" - The Self is the conqueror.

This shloka emphasizes the importance of self-control and inner strength in overcoming challenges and achieving success.

"Sarvam karmasu viniyogah" - All actions have consequences.

This shloka reminds us that our actions have consequences and that we should be mindful of how our actions impact ourselves and others.

CHAPTER EIGHTEEN

Moksa-Karmasu Kausalam

In Chapter 18 of the Bhagavad Gita, Krishna discusses the cause of liberation and bondage in action. He explains that actions have consequences and that one's actions can lead to either liberation or bondage.

Krishna teaches that actions performed with egoism, attachment, and desire bind one to the cycle of reincarnation, while actions performed without egoism, attachment, and desire lead to liberation. He advises that one should cultivate the qualities of detachment and selflessness in order to be free from the bonds of karma.

Krishna also discusses the nature of the three gunas, or qualities of nature, and how they influence one's actions and state of being. He explains that the quality of sattva, or goodness, leads to purity and enlightenment, while the qualities of rajas, or passion, and tamas, or ignorance, lead to ignorance and bondage.

In this chapter, Krishna advises Arjuna to cultivate the quality of sattva and to perform his duty selflessly, without attachment to the outcome. He teaches that this is the path to liberation and the realization of the supreme reality.

"Karmanye vadhikaraste ma phaleshu kadachana" (Bhagavad Gita 2.47) - "You have the right to perform your prescribed duty, but you are not entitled to the fruits of action." This shloka explains that we have a responsibility to perform our duties and responsibilities, but we should not be attached to the results or outcomes. Attachment to the fruits of action leads to bondage and suffering, while detachment from the fruits leads to liberation and peace.

"Niskarmasya yajñaõa karmaõi" (Bhagavad Gita 18.5) - "The work of one who is detached from the fruits of action is sacrifice." This shloka suggests that the ultimate form of action is selfless service, or work performed without any desire for personal gain or reward. When we perform actions with a sense of detachment and selflessness, we are able to transcend the cycle of action and reaction and attain liberation.

"Aparigrahaõa yajñaõa karmaõi" (Bhagavad Gita 18.9) - "The work of one who is free from attachment and egoism is sacrifice." This shloka emphasizes the importance of non-attachment in the pursuit of liberation. When we are attached to material possessions or egoistic desires, we become trapped in the cycle of action and reaction. However, when we cultivate a sense of non-attachment, we are able to perform actions without the burden of ego and achieve liberation.

"Sarvaõa karmasu kaunteya muktasangah samachara" (Bhagavad Gita 5.10) - "Perform all actions, O Arjuna, while remaining free from attachment and egoism." This shloka advises us to perform all actions with detachment and selflessness, recognizing that it is the actions themselves that are important, not the fruits of those actions. By following this advice, we can avoid becoming trapped in the cycle of action and reaction and instead achieve liberation.

Conclusion: A Summary Of The Key Teachings Of The Bhagavad Gita

The Bhagavad Gita is a Hindu scripture that is part of the epic poem Mahabharata. It is a conversation between the warrior prince Arjuna and the god Krishna, who serves as his charioteer and guide. The Gita is set on the battlefield of Kurukshetra, where Arjuna is faced with the moral dilemma of fighting against his own family and friends.

The Gita presents a philosophical and spiritual teaching on the nature of reality, the purpose of life, and the path to ultimate liberation. It presents the idea of karma yoga, or the path of action and selfless service, as the means to purifying the mind and attaining inner peace. It also teaches the importance of devotion to a personal god, or Bhakti yoga, as a means of realizing the ultimate reality.

The Gita also presents the idea of Jnana yoga, the path of knowledge and wisdom, and the ultimate goal as self-realization or attaining the state of being one with God. It also emphasizes the importance of being detached from the fruits of one's actions, and to act with a sense of duty and not attachment or aversion.

Overall, the Bhagavad Gita is a spiritual guidebook that teaches the importance of living a balanced, spiritual life and finding inner peace.

9 798889 518730

Printed by Libri Plureos GmbH in Hamburg,
Germany